Soft Toys

Cut out and sew your own original toys

SARA GERLINGS

ARCTURUS

To Nadine

Sara Gerlings was born in London and gained a BA (Hons) in Theatre Costume Design from Wimbledon School of Art. She has worked predominantly in the clothing industry but has also designed and made costumes for the Children's Shakespeare Company in south-west London. Sara has made toys since childhood. This collection demonstrates her signature choice of fabrics as an integral element of each toy's appearance and character.

Front cover projects:
Cat, Chinese ball and Tiny teddy
Back cover projects:
1 *Mouse* 2 *Alien* 3 *Chicken* 4 *Basket of fruit and vegetables* 5 *Snake*
6 *Russian doll* 7 *Mole* 8 *Elephant* 9 *Pig* 10 *Rabbit snuggler*

ARCTURUS

This edition published in 2012 by Arcturus Publishing Limited
26/27 Bickels Yard, 151–153 Bermondsey Street,
London SE1 3HA

Copyright © 2012 Arcturus Publishing Limited

ISBN: 978-1-84858-630-7
AD002116EN

Illustrated by David Woodroffe

Printed in China

CONTENTS

INTRODUCTION

Soft toys evoke many memories, and making your own can be a pleasurable extension to creating memories. When crafting your own toys, the greatest pleasure in production is watching the individual character of the toy evolve.

This book contains many new personalities waiting to come to life. Through the use of various fabrics, you will find a unique approach to soft toy-making, from the easy mouse to a medley of felt fruit and vegetables and up to more challenging items such as the Chinese ball. Each is labelled according to the skill level required, progressing through the book from the beginner to the more dextrous and adventurous sewer.

Chapters on equipment and materials, as well as methods and techniques, are included at the beginning of this book. Here you will find information and tips to help your new characters gain the most professional of finishes. The terminology used throughout is UK-standard, together with the relevant US terms alongside in square brackets [ ], which makes it a practical guide for all readers.

Each set of instructions states the dimensions of the toy fully made-up, along with the quantity of fabric you will need to replicate the finished toys shown in the cover photographs. If the original characters are not enough, there need be no limits to your imagination. By substituting fabrics in your own desired textures and colours, you can create a uniquely personal collection.

With the exception of three toys – the Alien, the Pig and the Russian Doll, whose original sizes require the pattern to be scaled up beforehand – the pattern grids can be used directly off the page to produce a toy of the stated size. However, the grid system means that you can work to any size you like when you follow the guide for scaling pattern pieces up or down. Once you have cut out your fabric, you will be ready to follow the illustrated step-by-step instructions and create some truly treasurable gifts, or perhaps a keepsake for yourself.

EQUIPMENT AND MATERIALS

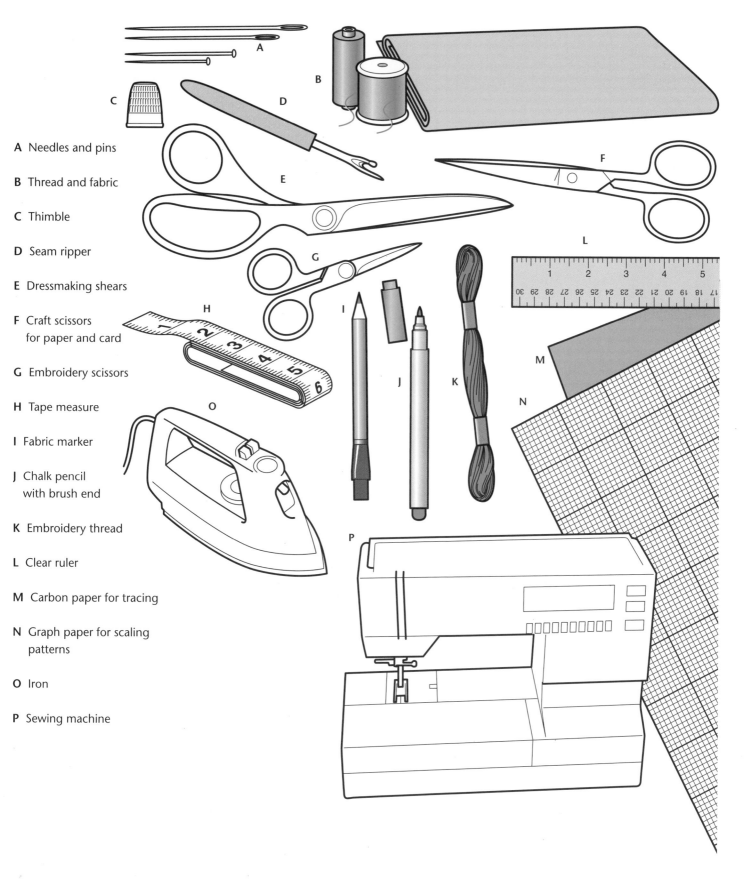

A Needles and pins

B Thread and fabric

C Thimble

D Seam ripper

E Dressmaking shears

F Craft scissors
   for paper and card

G Embroidery scissors

H Tape measure

I Fabric marker

J Chalk pencil
   with brush end

K Embroidery thread

L Clear ruler

M Carbon paper for tracing

N Graph paper for scaling
   patterns

O Iron

P Sewing machine

Fabrics, fillings and threads

EVERY WOVEN FABRIC BELONGS TO ONE OF THREE TYPES

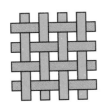

Plain weave Alternate warp (lengthwise) threads go over one and under one of the weft (crosswise) threads. Calico, lawn, organdy and taffeta are familiar examples.

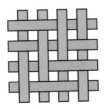

Twill weave Interlaces warp and weft threads over and under two or more threads progressively, weaving a clear diagonal pattern on durable fabrics like denim or gabardine.

Satin weave A smooth, glossy, compact surface created by long silky 'floats' that leave no weft visible; the reverse is matt.

FELT

A non-woven, non-fraying fabric, ideal for toy-making and for adding details like eyes and noses. Made from compressed fibres, good-quality felt contains a percentage of real wool. It comes in many bright colours, although direct sunlight may cause fading over time. Felt can be sewn or glued to other fabric.

GRAIN

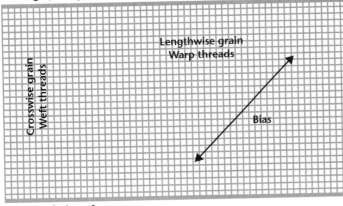

The grain of a woven fabric is the direction in which the warp and weft threads lie. The warp runs lengthwise, parallel to the selvedge [selvage]; this is the lengthwise grain. The weft follows the crosswise grain, at right angles to the selvedge [selvage].

The nap of a fabric is linked to the grain. Surfaces with a pile, like velvet and corduroy, can be smoothed one way and brushed up in the other, along the lengthwise grain.

FILLINGS

The most commonly used filling, polyester hollow fibre is springy, washable and hypoallergenic. Kapok is a soft natural plant fibre but not washable. Both are preferable to the lumpy results given by using ordinary cotton wool or chopped-up old tights [pantyhose]. Foam chips should never be used as toy filling because tiny particles of foam present a choking hazard to children.

BIAS

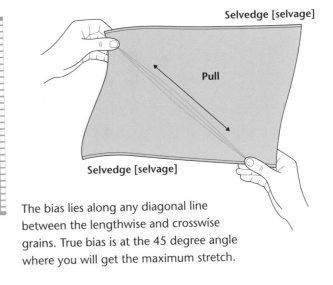

The bias lies along any diagonal line between the lengthwise and crosswise grains. True bias is at the 45 degree angle where you will get the maximum stretch.

THREADS

Like cloth, sewing thread can be natural or man-made, or combine the two. Silk (an animal fibre) is best for sewing woollens and silks. Cotton thread matches linen, cotton and rayon (all plant fibres); it hasn't much 'give' in it and is best used on a tightly woven fabric. Pure cotton has largely been replaced by cotton-covered polyester, where a polyester core provides strength and stretchability while the outer layer of mercerised cotton makes it smooth to work with. By contrast, nylon (polyamide) and polyester threads stretch and recover well, so they are suited to synthetic and knit fabrics.

Button thread is a useful tough thread for craftwork. Embroidery threads – both stranded cotton [floss] and perle [pearl] twist – are ideal for sewing faces and hair. Knitting yarn and rug wool also make realistic hair.

METHODS AND TECHNIQUES

Transferring patterns to fabric

From book page to paper or card Unless otherwise indicated, the patterns in this book are based on a 15 mm [⁹⁄₁₆ in] grid, i.e. exactly as it appears on the page. Using the pattern pieces without enlargement or reduction should produce a toy of the size stated at the top of the instructions.

To obtain same-size pattern pieces, photocopy the relevant page(s) or make a detailed tracing and then carefully cut out the paper

shapes with craft scissors. Each pattern piece includes the seam allowance and orange dots indicate contrast fabric.

However, you can also make these toys to your own specifications, for example, a much larger teddy based on the given grid (p. 47) or a family of small dolls (pp. 26–7). To enlarge or reduce one of the patterns, photocopy or scan the grid(s) to the required size and cut out the individual pieces from there.

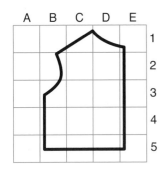

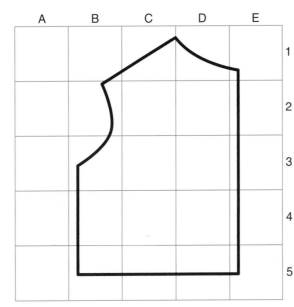

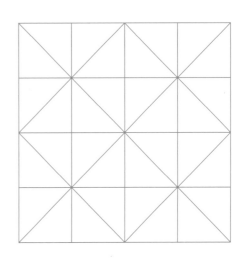

Scaling a grid pattern Alternatively, on a sheet of graph paper mark a new grid with the same number of squares, but larger or smaller as desired. Next, select a starting point and following the printed pattern square by square, copy the outline, pausing to check as you go. Include all the lettered points, the placing of ears and tails, and any nap direction. Do not forget to mark the gaps where you will insert the filling. Some people find it helps to superimpose diagonals on the basic grids, which provide more reference points for copying.

At this stage, if you are making several toys from the same pattern, it's a good idea to mount the uncut paper onto light card; cereal box cardboard is ideal. Whether using paper alone, or having mounted it onto card first, cut out each pattern piece carefully with craft scissors.

From paper or card to fabric Take your fabric and fold or place two layers wrong sides (WS) together on a firm, flat surface. When the pattern says 'cut two', cutting your pieces double like this will ensure you have two mirror-image shapes. When instructed to 'cut four', cut two pairs.

Use a fabric marker to trace round the card templates you have made; otherwise, pin the paper pattern piece directly to the fabric. Take care to note which way the grain, bias or nap should run and – most importantly – which edges should be placed on the fold of the fabric. If working with a strongly patterned fabric, ensure that it matches where necessary at the seams.

Cut the fabric out with dressmaker's shears. Smaller details such as the mouse's ears can be cut out with embroidery scissors. Don't allow anyone (including yourself) to blunt [dull] your dressmaker's shears or embroidery scissors by using them on paper or card.

Using a sewing machine

Although it is possible to sew any of these patterns by hand, some are more demanding than others and with fabrics such as close-woven cotton and corduroy, the best results are achieved by machine. Non-fraying fabrics like felt or fleece can be oversewn or blanket stitched by hand (p. 48) on the wrong side (WS) with

a very small seam allowance, which makes for a neat, firm finish. For a similar effect, the same fabrics should be machined with a straight stitch, not a zigzag. Use the longest stitches (4–6 mm) for heavyweight fabrics. Medium-length stitches (2.5–4 mm) are suitable for mid-weights and fine fabrics use a 2 mm stitch.

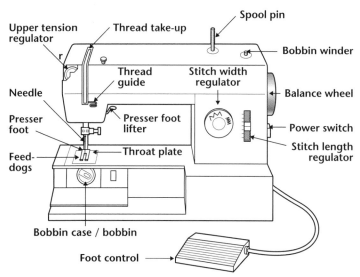

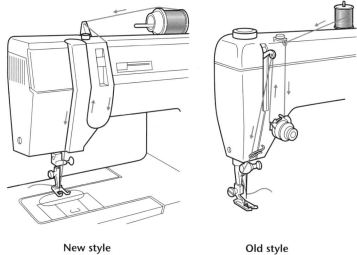

New style **Old style**

Regularly clear fluff [lint] from the feed-dogs and bobbin area. Avoid bent needles by raising the needle high before removing your work and don't drag on it while stitching. Always raise the presser foot while threading the machine and lower it when you put the machine away. Switch power off completely before disconnecting plugs, cleaning or attempting repairs.

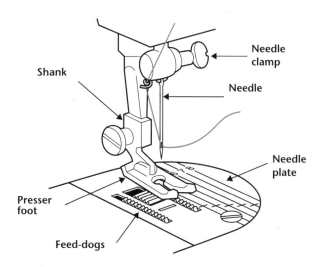

Threading the machine New-style machines incorporate the tension discs, thread guides and take-up lever inside their casings, avoiding various steps involved with threading older models. Note some needles thread from front to back and some from left to right. Incorrect threading is probably responsible for more beginners' problems than anything else. If you have no printed instructions, search for your make and model on the web, where a wide range of manuals is available.

Needle, presser foot, feed-dogs, needle plate General-purpose machine needles come in sizes 60–120 [8–19]. The finest will stitch delicates and the thickest will cope with tough fabrics like denim. Fit a ballpoint needle for knits or stretch fabrics. Needles will eventually go blunt [dull] or break, so keep spares and change them often. The presser foot holds the fabric flat against the feed-dogs while the needle makes the stitch. The feed-dogs have tiny metal teeth that move the fabric from front to back as the stitching proceeds. The needle plate fits over the feed-dogs, covering the bobbin, with a hole for the tip of the needle to pass through.

The bobbin A small metal reel holds the lower thread on a sewing machine. It lies next to the needle plate, in a compartment with a sliding lid. Lower thread tension is controlled by a small screw that regulates the spring on the bobbin case. Some bobbins operate clockwise and others anticlockwise – consult the manufacturer's manual.

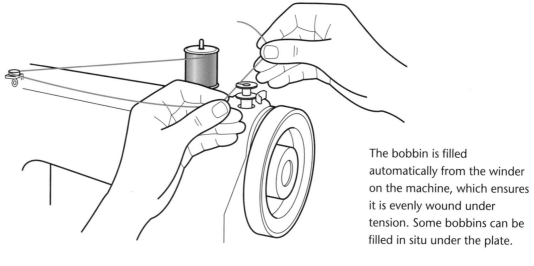

The bobbin is filled automatically from the winder on the machine, which ensures it is evenly wound under tension. Some bobbins can be filled in situ under the plate.

This type sits vertically in the bobbin race and is released by a latch on the case. When replaced, the thread should slot under the spring with a tail of 10 cm [4 in].

The 'drop-in' type sits horizontally beneath the lid. There is usually an angled slot to pull the bobbin thread through.

Assembling the toys

Before final stitching, by hand or machine, the pattern pieces should be pinned and tacked [basted] together according to the instructions given for individual toys.

Pile fabrics like velvet or corduroy need especially firm tacking [basting] with right sides (RS) together; the occasional backstitch (p. 48) will help too. This should prevent the layers from shifting

out of alignment while going through the machine. Velvet takes a stitch length of 2–2.5 mm with a loosened upper thread tension, using a 75–90 [11–14] needle. Practice on offcuts if you have never sewn velvet before. As you stitch, hold the bottom layer taut without dragging on the needle. A quilting or 'walking' foot copes with pile fabrics by feeding upper and lower layers together evenly.

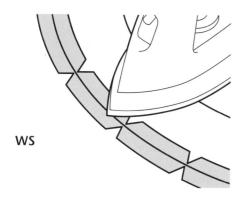

WS

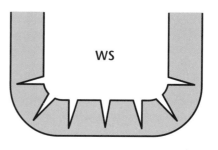

WS

Clipping outward curves Curved seams naturally give rise to curved seam allowances, which have to be clipped to allow them to stretch or fold together neatly and lie flat. If you have to clip down to the stitch line, be careful not to cut the stitching itself. If necessary afterwards, use the tip of the iron to smooth any puckers.

Clipping inward curves Single cuts at regular intervals may be enough to ease together silk or cotton lawn, but to avoid bulking up on thicker fabrics, cut wedge-shaped notches into the seam allowance and remove the excess completely.

Safety eyes and joints

Turning and filling the toys

 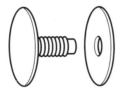

Safety eyes Attach these before filling and closing the toy. Be sure that you have the correct eye position beforehand because once fixed they are impossible to remove. Make a very small hole in the fabric with your embroidery scissors and push the post section of the eye through from front to back. To avoid scratching it, rest the eye, post upwards, on a padded surface and push the washer down firmly over the post.

Disc joints For a scaled-up teddy with moveable limbs, each joint will consist of the main disc and post, a second plain disc, and a washer. (See p. 47 for details of attachment)

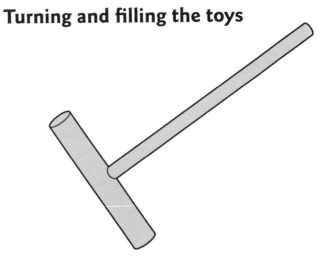

Stuffing stick Having checked that all seams are properly finished, turn the toy RS out through the filling gap, starting with the narrowest extremities. Smooth seamlines from the inside with the top of a knitting needle; don't use anything sharp. Start filling the tips of limbs, noses and so on, packing them firmly so they won't sag where they meet the body. A T-shaped stuffing stick made from wooden dowel can help.

Hairstyles

Short hairstyles

Plaits and bunches

Grandad-style hair and moustache

Long hair

Looped hair

The Russian doll (pp. 26–28) is a very basic shape and capable of many variations – simple or elaborate. Here are some ideas for hairstyles for different characters, including a grandad with a droopy moustache. To create an impression of curls, use ordinary thread to stitch down a series of loops. The girl's plaits are worked from loose strands stitched into a centre parting, then caught down again with a few firm stitches at cheek-level.

Rug wool, double knitting [Worsted] and baby wool are all suitable yarns for hair, depending on the size of the doll. Embroidery threads look good on very small heads and can be used for the facial features as well.

Trimmings

BEADS

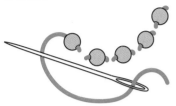 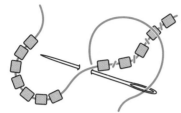

Working with a fine milliner's needle, secure the sewing cotton with two small stitches on the spot, then thread on the first bead. Insert the needle near the starting stitches. Advance one stitch and bring the needle through ready for the next bead.

Thread up two needles and secure both threads as before. Thread the first needle with the desired number of beads. With the second needle, stitch over the first thread coming through the first bead – this is known as couching. Slide the second bead close to the first and repeat until all the beads are in place.

SEQUINS

Secure the sewing cotton with two small stitches on the spot and bring the needle up through the eye of the first sequin. Back stitch over the right-hand edge, come out on the left-hand edge and back stitch down through the eye. Advance a stitch and repeat with the next sequin.

Secure the thread as before and bring the needle up through the eye of the first sequin. Thread on one small bead before re-inserting the needle through the same eye. Pull firmly to bring bead into contact with sequin. Advance one stitch on wrong side and bring needle up through eye of next sequin.

CORD-MAKING

This technique takes practice. Cut two lengths of rayon or metallic embroidery thread, four times as long as the desired cord. Knot the threads together at both ends and ask someone to hold one end while you slot a pencil through the other. Pull the loop taut between you and start twisting the pencil. Eventually, the cord will curl up as you relax the tension. Place a finger halfway and let go of one end, allowing it to twist on itself to form the full cord. Roll out any kinks with your thumb and forefinger. Tie ends in a knot.

TASSELS

 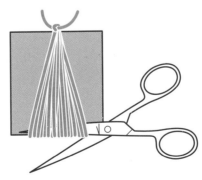 

1 Wrap the yarn or embroidery thread around a piece of card that measures about 1 cm [½ in] more than the desired tassel length. Thread one strand, 30 cm [12 in] long, under the top loops.

2 Tie this strand tightly at the top; the ends can be knotted or crocheted later, or threaded up for sewing. Cut all the tassel loops free at the lower edge.

3 Take another length of yarn or thread and wind firmly round the loose strands to form the tassel head. Finish with a secure knot. Thread the ends into a needle and work them neatly into the centre of the tassel before trimming level.

MOUSE

LENGTH: 10 cm [4 in]   LEVEL: BEGINNER

YOU WILL NEED

Fabric 25 x 15 cm
[10 x 6 in] for the body –
felt is ideal

Scraps of felt for the ears

60 cm [24 in] embroidery
thread for the tail

Filling

Cut out all the pattern pieces.

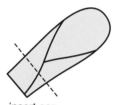

insert ear
into slit

1 Cut ear slits in each side from C to D. Fold ears in on themselves and insert into the slits on each of the body sides.

2 Thread a needle with a double length of ordinary sewing cotton or a single strand of perle [pearl] embroidery thread. Knot the end of the thread.

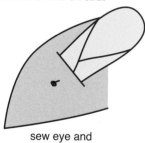

sew eye and
secure ear

3 Needle through from the wrong side (WS), then stitch once or twice through the body and ear. Bring the needle out on the right side (RS) and make a French knot (p. 48) to create the eye.

4 Repeat for the other side.

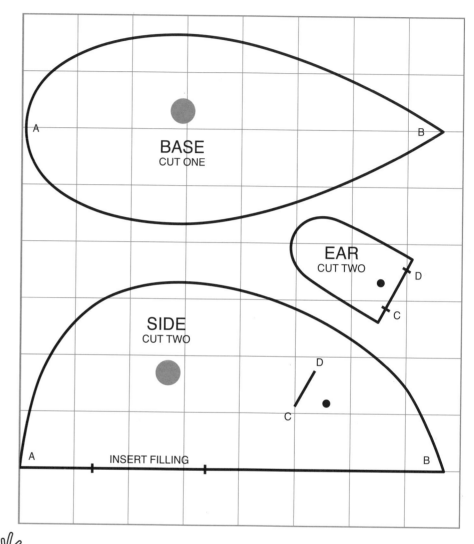

BASE
CUT ONE

EAR
CUT TWO

SIDE
CUT TWO

INSERT FILLING

5 Cut three 20 cm [8 in] strands of embroidery thread for the tail. Tie a knot in one end and plait as far as you wish before tying off with a knot and leaving a tassel end.

6 Place the body sides RS (with ears) together and stitch the spine from B to A. If sewing felt, you need little seam allowance and could use a small blanket stitch (p. 48).

7 Insert the base section and sew up one side from nose (B) to tail (A).

8 Insert the tail centrally on the back seam with only the base knot sticking

out. The rest of the tail should be inside the mouse for now.

9 Sew up the other side, leaving a gap for turning and filling.

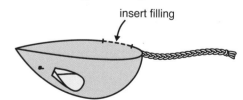

insert filling

10 Turn the mouse body RS out and insert the filling firmly to form the full body shape.

11 Close the gap neatly with slip stitch.

ALIEN

HEIGHT: 32 cm [12½ in]   **LEVEL: BEGINNER**

Note: This pattern is two-thirds of the original size. For a full-size alien you need to scale up to a 22.5 mm [8⅞ in] grid (p. 7).

YOU WILL NEED

Fabric 80 x 30 cm
[32 x 12 in] for the body
– a close-woven cotton
is best

Two buttons for the eyes

Filling

Cut out both pattern pieces. There is a 5 mm [3⁄16 in] seam allowance.

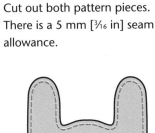

1 Place right sides (RS) together and sew right round the figure from side to side of the gap marked for turning and filling.

2 Clip the curves in the seam allowance (p. 9).

3 Turn the alien to the RS.

4 Iron out any puckers around the edge.

5 Insert the filling firmly, using a stuffing stick to reach all the narrow extremities.

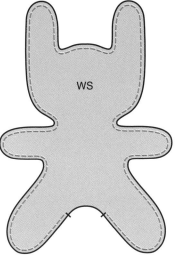

6 Close the gap neatly with slip stitch.

7 Sew on buttons for the eyes.

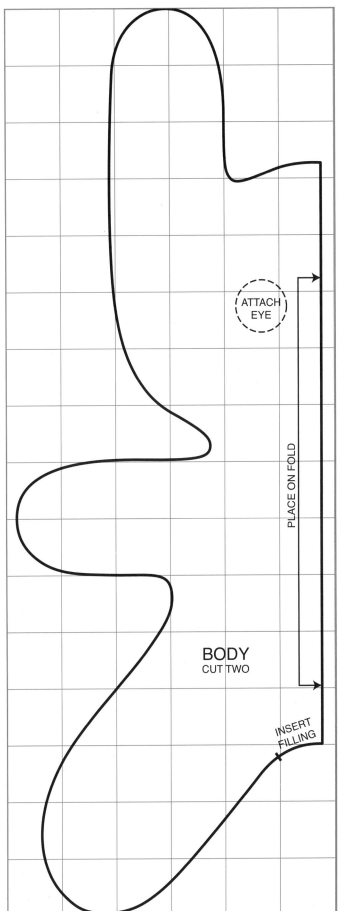

CHICKEN

HEIGHT: 30 cm [12 in] INCLUDING LEGS: 52 cm [20½ in]   LEVEL: INTERMEDIATE

YOU WILL NEED

Yellow towelling fabric 70 x 40 cm [27½ x 15¾ in] for the body, wings and feet

Red towelling fabric 50 x 25 cm [19⅝ x 9¾ in] for the legs, comb and wattle

Two large buttons for the eyes

Filling

Cut out all the pattern pieces. There is a 5 mm [³⁄₁₆ in] seam allowance.

1 Place the wings right sides (RS) together and sew round from A to B, leaving the flat side open.

2 Turn the wings RS out.

3 Place wattle RS together and sew round from G to H, leaving the flat side open.

4 Turn the wattle RS out.

5 Take the square of body fabric, place RS up and pleat one corner as shown, tacking [basting] the wings and wattle

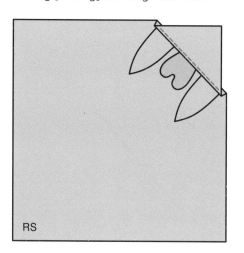

into the fold to a depth of 15 mm [⁵⁄₈ in]. Continuing RS up, hem along the fold, ensuring the needle goes through all the layers to hold everything in place at the neck line.

6 Place comb RS together and sew round from C to D, leaving the flat side open.

7 Turn comb RS out.

8 Fold the body RS together from the beak point, joining J to I.

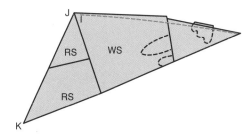

9 Tack [baste] the comb into the back seam line with the taller end nearest the beak point. Then sew the back seam.

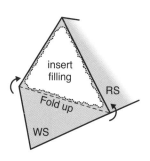

10 Turn RS out and fill generously. Fold up the triangular base section and slip stitch round the two open sides to close the body with K meeting J/I.

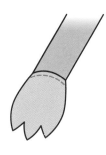

11 Place feet right sides (RS) together and sew round each from E to F, leaving the flat side open. Turn feet RS out.

12 Fold the legs RS together and seam up both to form tubes. Turn the legs RS out.

13 Turn raw edges under at tops of feet and sew each foot to the end of one leg.

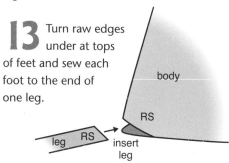

14 Poke the front corners of the body in on themselves and insert the top of a leg into each. Pin and tack [baste] to ensure the legs are even and attach them by slip stitching in a straight line across the body corners.

15 Sew the buttons back-to-back either side of the beak, just below the comb.

16 With black thread, stab stitch through the top fold of the beak, just ahead of the comb, and make French knots on either side to mark the chicken's nostrils.

A   B

WING
CUT FOUR

L   L

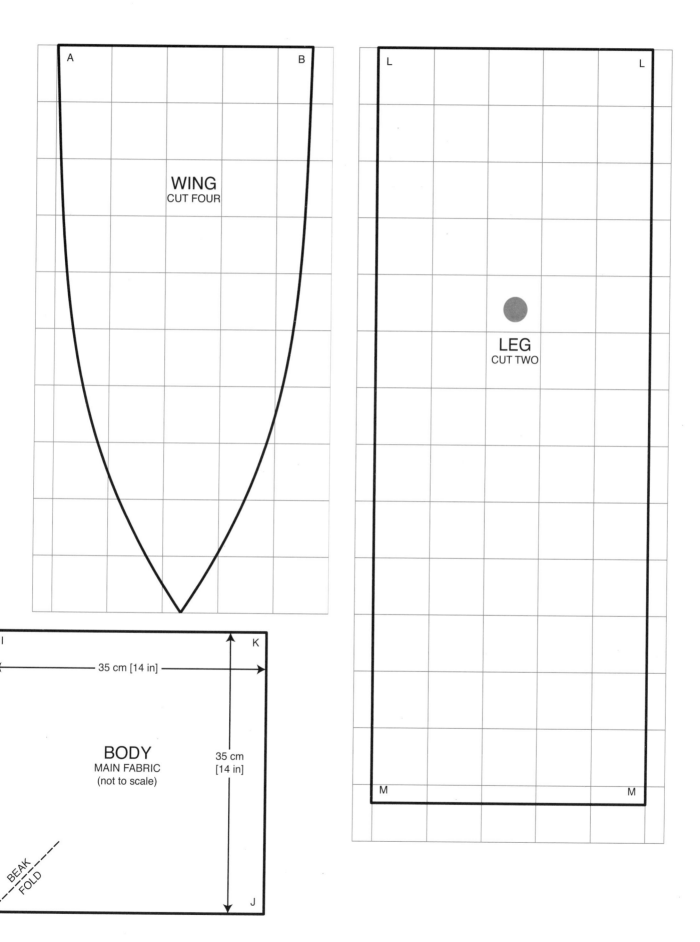

LEG
CUT TWO

I   K

←———— 35 cm [14 in] ————→

BODY
MAIN FABRIC
(not to scale)

35 cm
[14 in]

BEAK
FOLD

J

M   M

CHICKEN

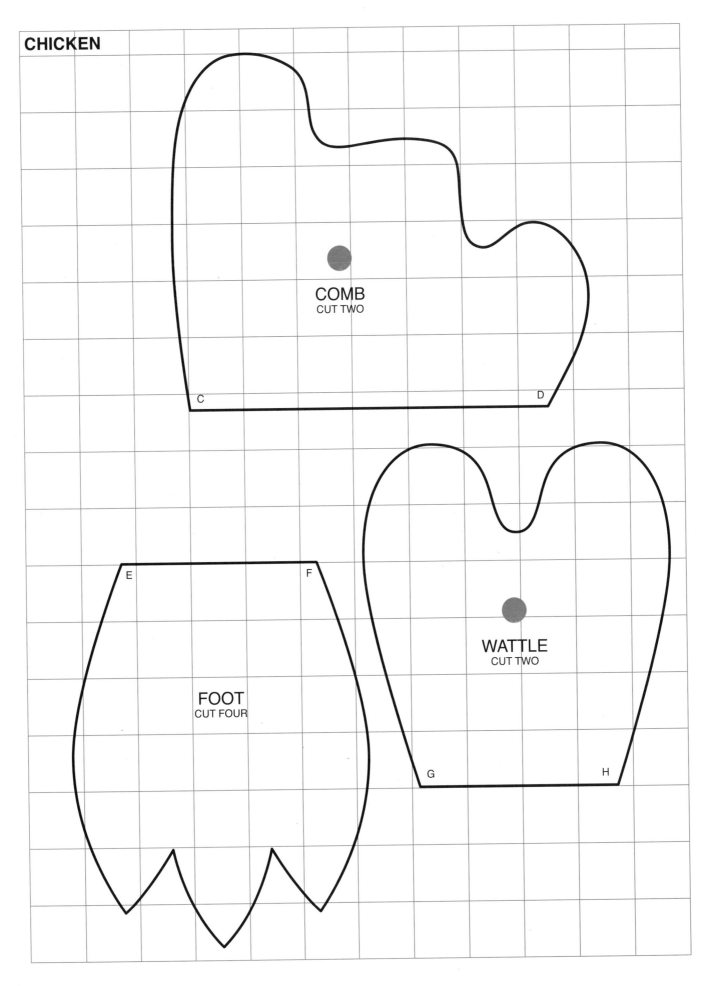

COMB
CUT TWO

C   D

WATTLE
CUT TWO

E   F

FOOT
CUT FOUR

G   H

BASKET

SIZE: 12 cm [4¾ in] CUBE   LEVEL: BEGINNER

YOU WILL NEED

Thick brown felt
50 x 36 cm [20 x 14½ in]

Piece of medium card
12 cm [4¾ in] square
for base

Spraying with water-based hat stiffener
is optional. Cut the felt into 9 strips of
50 x 4 cm [19⅝ x 1⅝ in] and for guidance
mark the centre point of each on one side
with a chalk marker.

1 Lay the strips on a firm surface with the
chalk marks visible. Start weaving them
from the centre outwards, as shown.

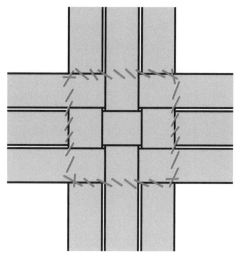

2 Interweave six strips, pull them closely
together, then tack [baste] around the
base area, being sure to stitch each strip to
its neighbour.

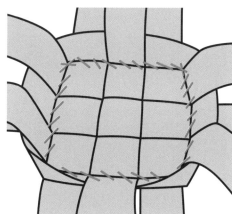

3 Take one of the remaining three
strips. Starting at a point that will be
concealed from the outside, bend the base
strips up vertically and begin weaving the
sides. One strip will weave one round of the
basket. When complete, overlap the ends
and tack [baste] to hold in place.

4 Repeat twice more, taking care to
start and finish each strip where it
won't show.

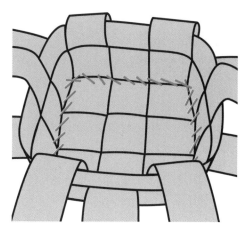

5 Take each vertical strip in turn and fold
over to the inside of the basket. Glue
down and trim the ends level. Alternatively,
tack [baste] and back stitch around the
top layer, 1 cm [½ in] from the top edge.
Remove all tacking [basting]

6 Fit the card square into the base of the
basket. Use glue sparingly if required.
Add four more card squares to the interior
sides for a rigid box.

CARROT

HEIGHT: 10 cm [4 in] INCLUDING LEAVES: 17 cm [6⅝ in]   LEVEL: BEGINNER

YOU WILL NEED

Orange felt 15 cm [6 in] square

Scraps of mixed green felt for the leaves

Filling

Cut out all the pattern pieces.

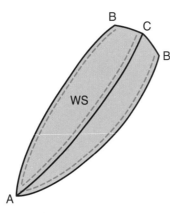

1 Sew two orange sections together from A to B and the third from A to C. When sewing felt, you need little seam allowance and could use a small blanket stitch (p. 48).

2 Stitch the remaining seam and turn the carrot right side out.

3 Insert the filling at the top of the carrot and stuff firmly right to the tip.

4 Secure all the carrot leaves together with a couple of stitches at one end.

5 Running stitch around the top of the carrot, tuck the leaves inside and gather the running stitch in as tightly as possible to hold them together.

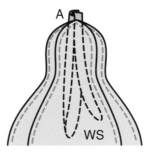

6 Wrap the thread twice around the top and back stitch two or three times before tying off.

PEAR

HEIGHT: 8 cm [3⅛ in]   LEVEL: BEGINNER

YOU WILL NEED

Mid-green felt 20 cm [8 in] square

Scraps of brown felt for the leaves

Filling

Cut out all the pattern pieces.

1 Sew two of the six green sections together from A to B.

2 Take one more section and sew from A to B again.

3 Repeat so that there are two halves to the pear.

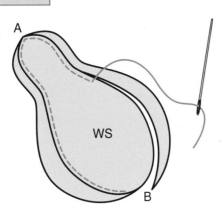

4 Take the two brown leaves and insert them upside down between the two halves, ensuring that all the points A are lined up before stitching all together.

5 Sew the two halves of the pear body together, leaving a gap for filling at the base.

6 Turn the pear right side out.

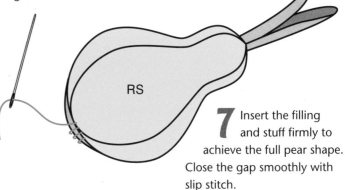

7 Insert the filling and stuff firmly to achieve the full pear shape. Close the gap smoothly with slip stitch.

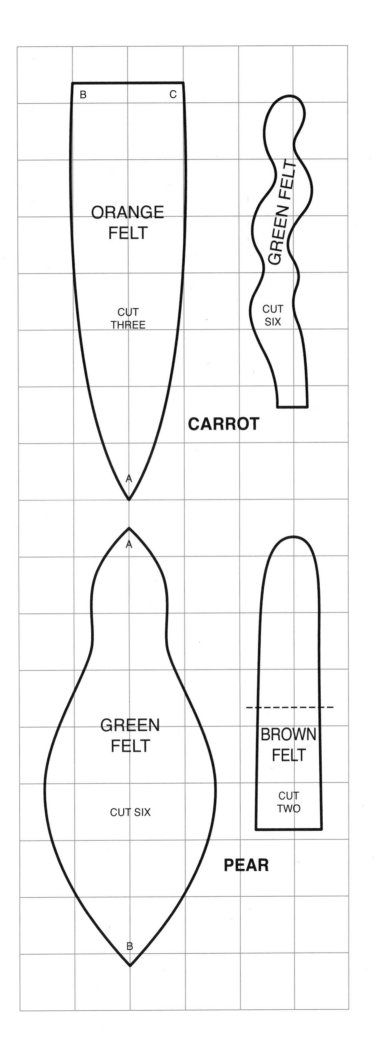

ORANGE
FELT

CUT
THREE

GREEN FELT

CUT
SIX

B   C

A

CARROT

A

GREEN
FELT

CUT SIX

BROWN
FELT

CUT
TWO

B

PEAR

RED FELT

CUT SIX

TOMATO

CUT TWO

GREEN FELT

GREEN FELT

CUT ONE

WHITE FELT

CUT TWO

A

B

APPLE

A

B

ORANGE

ORANGE FELT

CUT ONE

A

B

YELLOW FELT

CUT TWO

A

B

ORANGE

LENGTH: 6 cm [2⅜ in]   **LEVEL: BEGINNER**

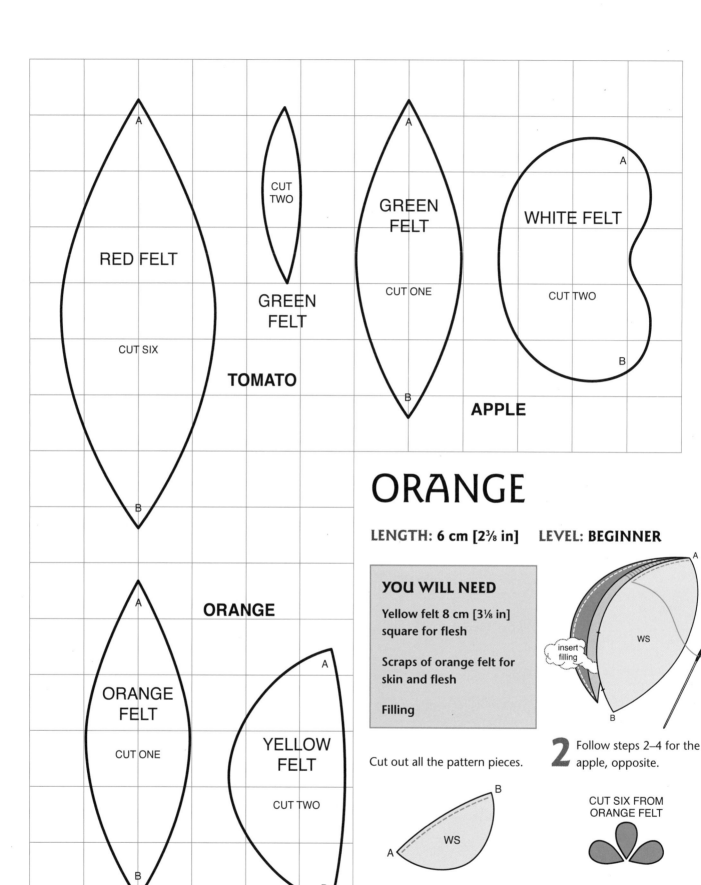

YOU WILL NEED

Yellow felt 8 cm [3⅛ in] square for flesh

Scraps of orange felt for skin and flesh

Filling

Cut out all the pattern pieces.

2 Follow steps 2–4 for the apple, opposite.

WS

insert filling

A

B

WS

1 Sew the two yellow sections together from A to B on the straight side.

CUT SIX FROM ORANGE FELT

3 Glue or stitch three appliqué shapes to each side of the segment.

TOMATO

HEIGHT: 5.5 cm [2⅛ in]   **LEVEL: BEGINNER**

YOU WILL NEED

Red felt 20 cm [8 in] square

Scraps of dark green felt for leaves

Filling

Cut out all the pattern pieces.

1 Sew two of the six red sections together from A to B.

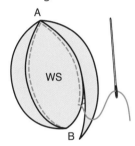

2 Take one more section and sew from A to B again.

3 Repeat so that there are two halves to the tomato.

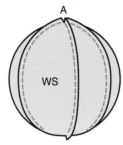

4 Line up the six points at A before stitching all together.

5 Sew the two halves of the tomato together, leaving a gap for filling.

6 Turn right side out.

7 Insert enough to achieve a well-rounded shape. Close the gap with slip stitch but leave a thread about 30 cm [12 in] long.

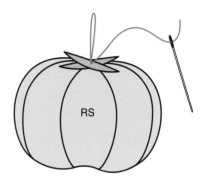

8 Take the four leaves and place in a cross on top of the tomato. Bring the long thread up through the filling to the top and through the four leaves. Make a small stitch at the centre of the leaves as you take the thread back down again through the tomato and out at the base.

9 Repeat twice more, pulling firmly on the thread to produce the authentic tomato shape before tying off.

APPLE

LENGTH: 6 cm [2⅜ in]   **LEVEL: BEGINNER**

YOU WILL NEED

White felt 8 cm [3⅛ in] square for flesh

Scraps of light green felt for skin and brown for pips

Filling

Cut out all pattern pieces.

1 Sew the two white flesh sections together from A to B on the wavy side.

2 Sew one side of the green skin section from A to B on the remaining free side of one of the white sections.

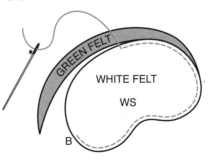

3 Sew the other side of the green section to the remaining free side of the other white section.

4 Turn right side out and insert the filling. Close the gap with slip stitch.

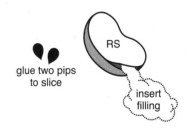

glue two pips to slice

5 Cut two pips using the shapes given here. Glue or stitch to either side of the slice.

LETTUCE

HEIGHT: 8 cm [3⅛ in]   LEVEL: BEGINNER

Cut out all the pattern pieces.

1 Construct the lettuce heart from yellow felt, following the steps for the tomato (p. 21) as far as filling and closing with slip stitch.

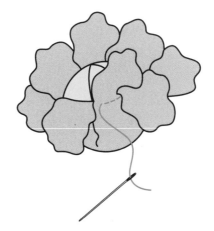

3 Wrap the leaves around the yellow heart and attach with running stitch to the central ball shape.

6 Line up all points C and sew the two halves together to form a frilled cup shape.

7 Fit the previous lettuce into the new 'cup' and slip stitch the new leaves to the former outer leaves, which are now pressed more closely round the heart.

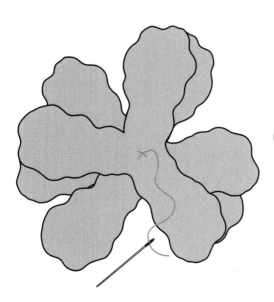

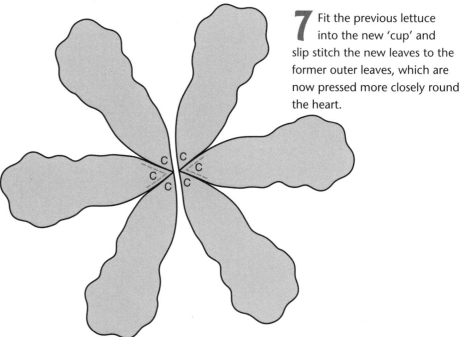

2 Take the four triple-leafed pieces, layer them and fan them out into a circle. Stitch them together in the centre.

4 Take three remaining single leaves and, starting at points C, sew them together along half their lengths, as if they were sections of a ball.

5 Repeat with the other three.

LETTUCE

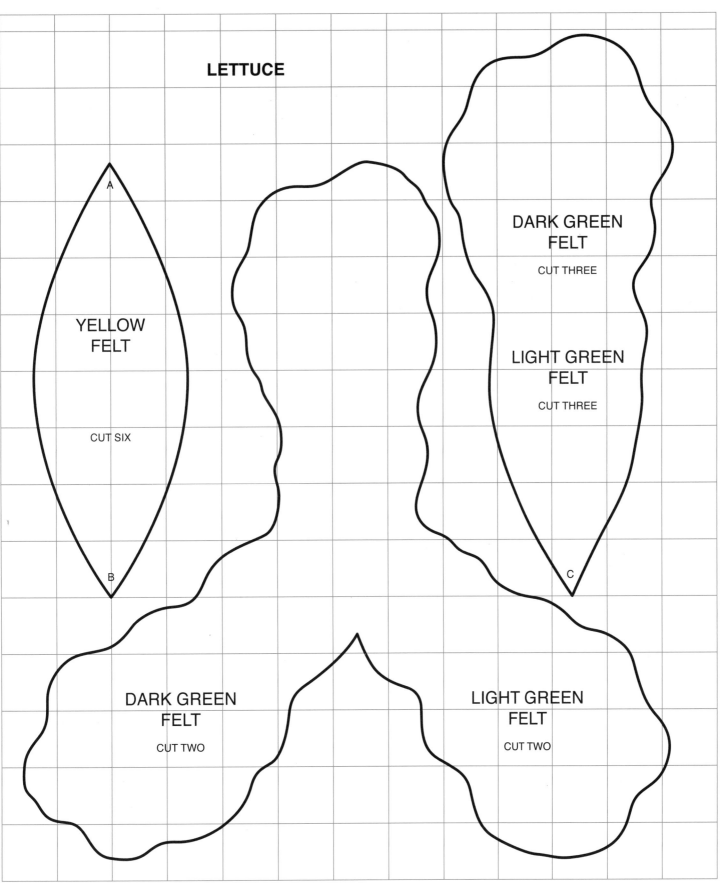

YELLOW
FELT

CUT SIX

A

B

DARK GREEN
FELT

CUT THREE

LIGHT GREEN
FELT

CUT THREE

C

DARK GREEN
FELT

CUT TWO

LIGHT GREEN
FELT

CUT TWO

SNAKE

COILED HEIGHT: 14 cm [5½ in]   LEVEL: INTERMEDIATE

Note: Because of the tight spiral construction and the fact that the snake needs very firm filling, you are advised to use a sewing machine throughout.

YOU WILL NEED

Top fabric 50 x 20 cm [20 x 8 in] – a close-woven fabric is best

Contrast fabric 50 x 20 cm [20 x 8 in] – also close-woven

10 cm [4 in] ribbon or tape

A pair of beads or buttons for eyes

Filling

Cut out all the pattern pieces. There is a 5 mm [³⁄₁₆ in] seam allowance.

1 Take the four body rings and cut each one in half along the fold to produce eight sections (for a longer snake, simply increase the number of rings, remembering they work in pairs).

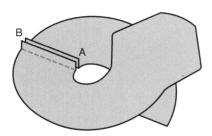

2 With right sides (RS) together, sew the top fabric head section to the first semi-circle at A and B.

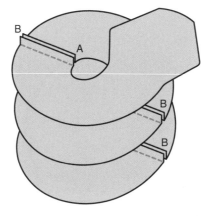

3 Carry on joining the remaining top fabric semi-circles at A and B to create a spiral.

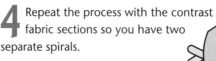

4 Repeat the process with the contrast fabric sections so you have two separate spirals.

5 Iron the seams to smooth out any puckers.

6 Pin and tack [baste] both spirals together, RS facing.

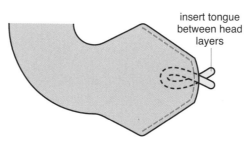

insert tongue between head layers

7 Loop and tack [baste] the snake's tongue to the front of its head with two ends protruding.

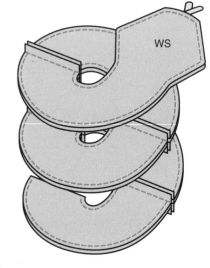

WS

8 Starting at the tongue, sew down each side of the snake.

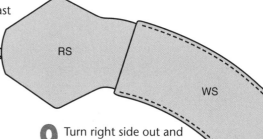

RS

WS

9 Turn right side out and stuff firmly from the open tail end, using a stuffing stick.

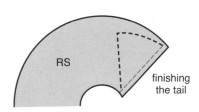

RS

finishing the tail

10 Tuck the tail in on itself, creating a 45 degree angle, and slip stitch the tail closed. Sew eyes to head at widest point.

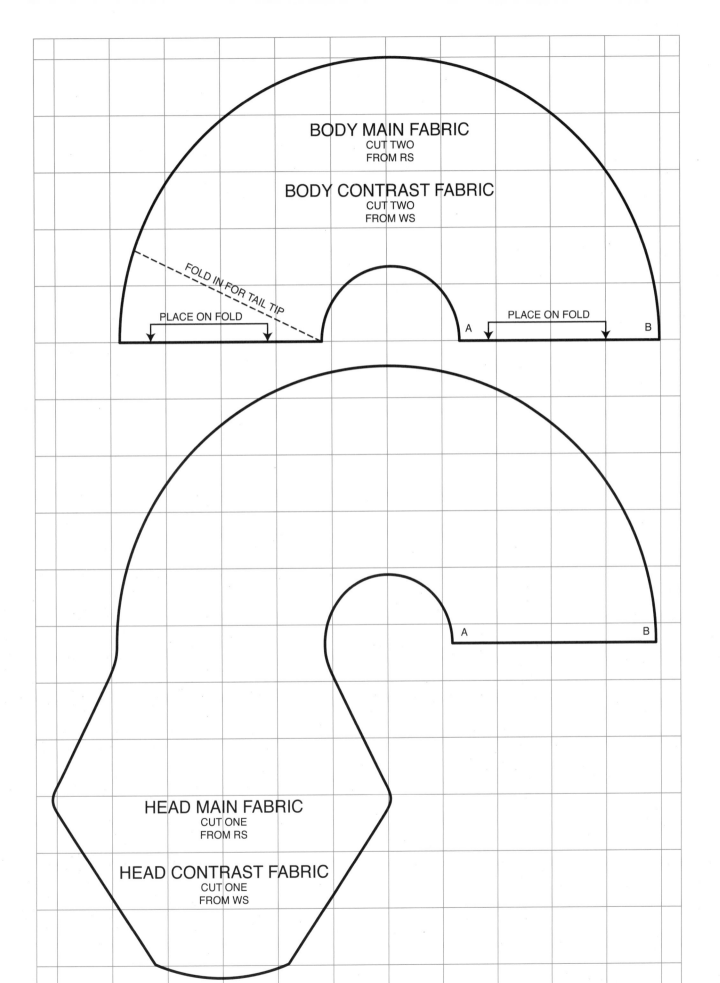

BODY MAIN FABRIC
CUT TWO
FROM RS

BODY CONTRAST FABRIC
CUT TWO
FROM WS

FOLD IN FOR TAIL TIP

PLACE ON FOLD

PLACE ON FOLD

A

B

HEAD MAIN FABRIC
CUT ONE
FROM RS

HEAD CONTRAST FABRIC
CUT ONE
FROM WS

A

B

RUSSIAN DOLL

HEIGHT: 28 cm [11 in]   LEVEL: INTERMEDIATE

Note: This pattern is two-thirds of the original size – for a full-size Russian doll you need to scale up to a 22.5 mm grid (p. 7). A simplified version for beginners uses two back sections in a neutral fabric such as unbleached calico, forming the basis for many other characters.

YOU WILL NEED

Fabric 45 x 40 cm [18 x 16 in] for main doll shape

White felt 20 cm [8 in] square for sleeves and face

Card 20 cm [8 in] square

Red embroidery thread for sleeve decoration

Embroidery thread in various colours for face and hair

Beads, braid, lace etc for trimmings

Filling

Cut out all the pattern pieces. There is a 5 mm [³⁄₁₆ in] seam allowance.

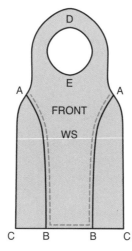

2 Attach both sleeves to the front body, tack [baste] and stitch from A to B on each side.

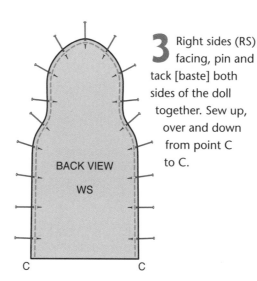

3 Right sides (RS) facing, pin and tack [baste] both sides of the doll together. Sew up, over and down from point C to C.

4 Turn RS out and stuff firmly before inserting first card disc at base.

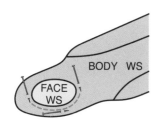

1 Pin and tack [baste] the face fabric in place on the front body section, matching points D and E. Then slip stitch into position, easing the fabric into the gap as you go.

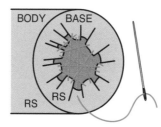

5 Gather the fabric as shown and hold the disc in place with long stitches from side to side. This is the inner base. Be sure to catch the fabric evenly all round, pulling it taut so that the doll stands upright.

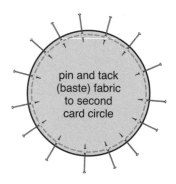

6 Take the circle of fabric and cover the second card disc, tacking [basting] the fabric to the card as shown. This is the outer base.

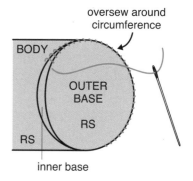

7 Oversew (p. 48) the outer base to the inner one and remove all tacking [basting].

8 Use red embroidery thread to decorate the sleeves in traditional Russian style with rows of simple cross stitch.

9 Embroider the face and hair using the grid pattern as a guide to placing the features.

10 Add any other trimmings such as beads, lace or braid as you wish.

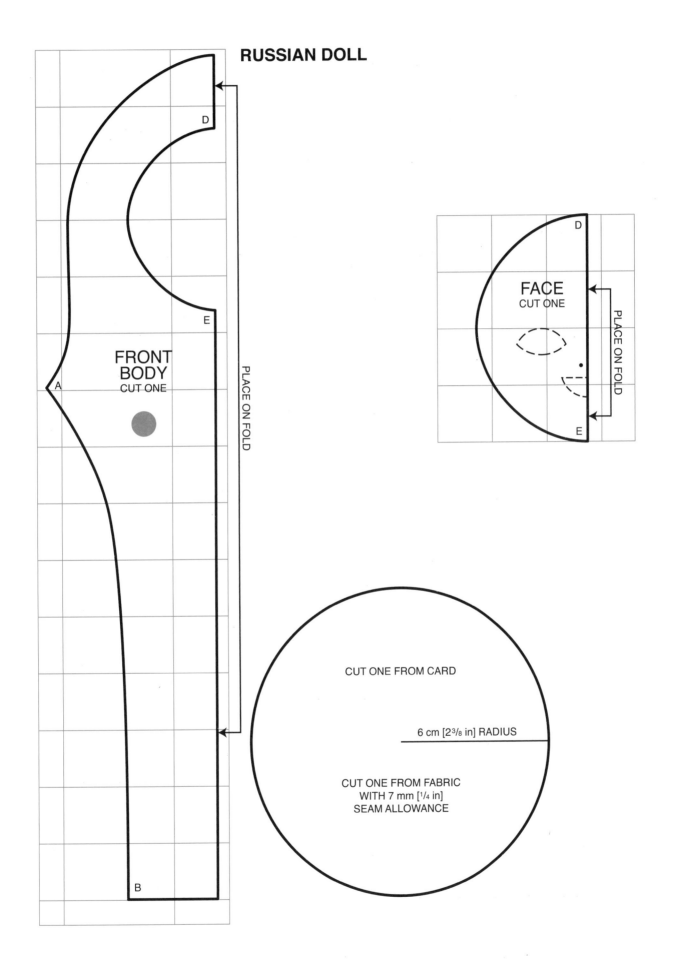

D

E

A

FRONT BODY
CUT ONE

PLACE ON FOLD

B

FACE
CUT ONE

D

E

PLACE ON FOLD

CUT ONE FROM CARD

6 cm [2³/₈ in] RADIUS

CUT ONE FROM FABRIC
WITH 7 mm [¹/₄ in]
SEAM ALLOWANCE

RUSSIAN DOLL

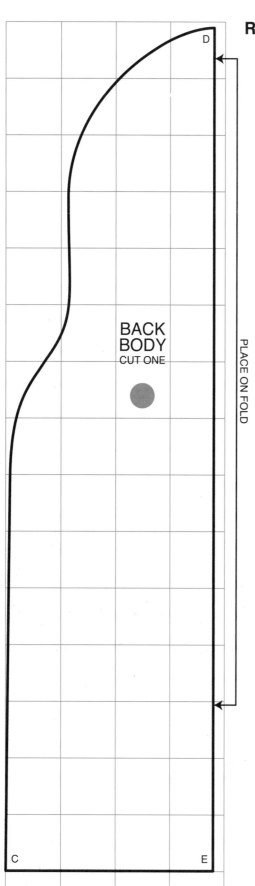

BACK BODY
CUT ONE

D

C E

PLACE ON FOLD

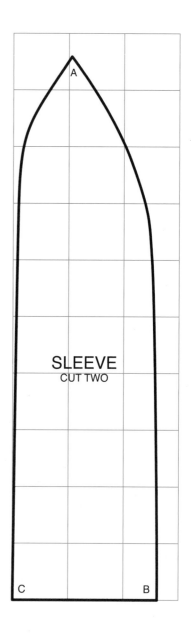

SLEEVE
CUT TWO

A

C B

MOLE

LENGTH: 17.5 cm [7 in]   **LEVEL: INTERMEDIATE**

YOU WILL NEED

Black velvet fabric
30 x 20 cm [12 x 8 in]
for the body

Pink corded velvet fabric
50 x 10 cm [20 x 4 in] for
the feet

Two two-holed mother-
of-pearl buttons for the
eyes

Filling

Cut out all the pattern pieces, ensuring
the nap direction matches on both body
pieces and feet. There is a 4 mm [⅛ in]
seam allowance.

1 Place right sides (RS) together and
with a 4 mm [⅛ in] seam allowance,
sew right round the four feet from A to B,
leaving the straight edge open for turning.

2 Turn the feet RS out.

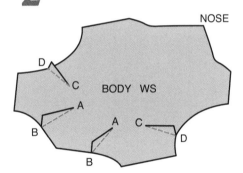

3 With a 4 mm [⅛ in] seam allowance,
tack [baste] and sew darts on the body
section, A to B and C to D.

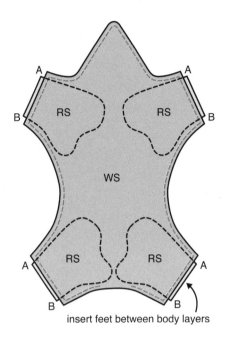

insert feet between body layers

4 Insert the feet into all four leg holes
and pin, making sure the 'thumbs' are
all facing towards the rear end of the mole's
body. Pin, tack [baste] and sew around the
mole's body, leaving a gap for turning and
filling at the rear end.

5 Turn the body RS out and fill.

6 Slip stitch the gap closed.

7 Sew buttons to the mole's face with
stitches at matching angles as shown.

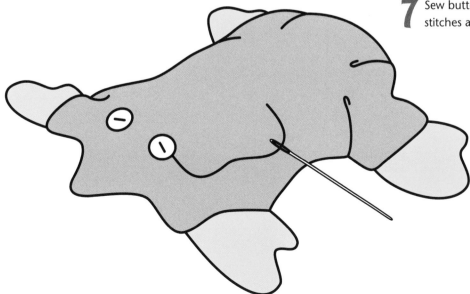

MOLE

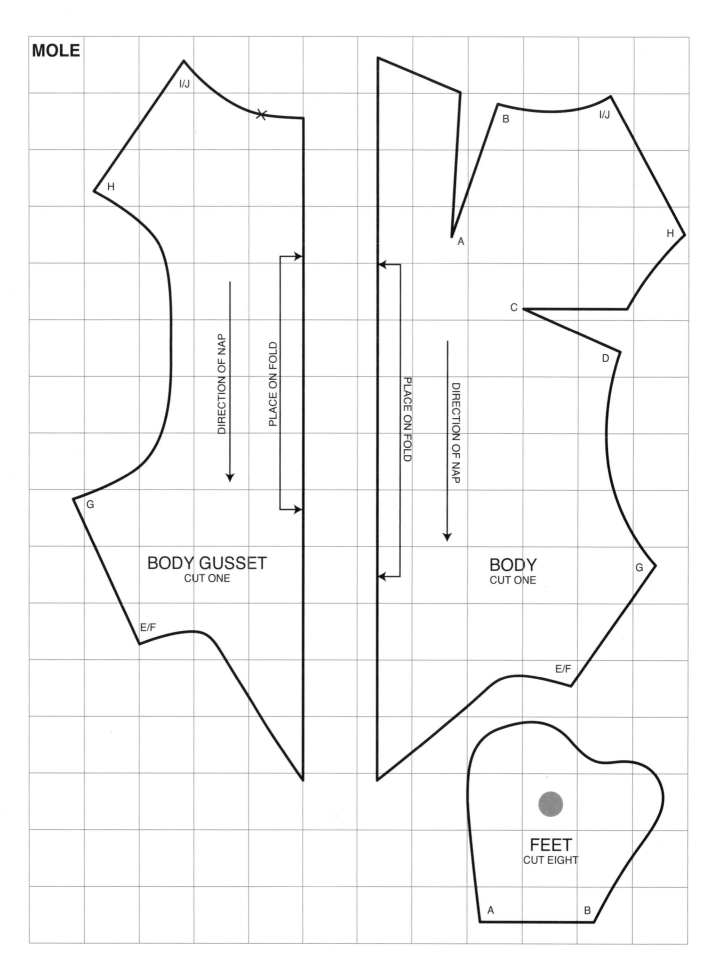

BODY GUSSET
CUT ONE

DIRECTION OF NAP

PLACE ON FOLD

PLACE ON FOLD

DIRECTION OF NAP

BODY
CUT ONE

FEET
CUT EIGHT

I/J

H

G

E/F

B

I/J

H

A

C

D

G

E/F

A

B

ELEPHANT

HEIGHT: 18 cm [7 in] **LENGTH:** 25.5 cm [10 in]   **LEVEL: ADVANCED**

Note: Because of the complex seaming required and the fact that the elephant needs very firm filling, you are advised to use a sewing machine throughout.

> **YOU WILL NEED**
>
> **Main body fabric 65 x 40 cm [25½ x 16 in] – close-woven is best**
>
> **Contrast fabric 65 x 25 cm [25½ x 10 in] for gussets and ear lining – close-woven is best**
>
> **60 cm [24 in] black embroidery thread for tail**
>
> **Two small black buttons for eyes**
>
> **Filling**

EAR
WS

K   L

Cut out all the pattern pieces. There is a 5 mm [³⁄₁₆ in] seam allowance.

1 In the contrast fabric, sew half the body gusset to the inner front and rear leg sections, from B to A and from C to D.

2 Repeat with the other half of the body gusset.

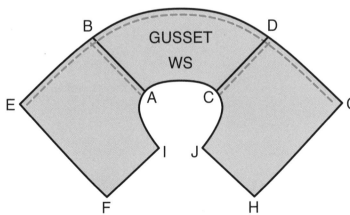

GUSSET
WS

B   D
E   A   C   G
        I   J
F   H

3 Pin and tack [baste] the two body gusset assemblies right sides (RS) together, then stitch from E to G. Clip the curve.

4 Take two ear pieces, one of each fabric, and place RS together. Tack [baste] and sew around the curve from K to L, leaving the straight side open for turning.

5 Repeat for the second ear. Clip the curves and turn both ears RS out.

Insert ears between head layers

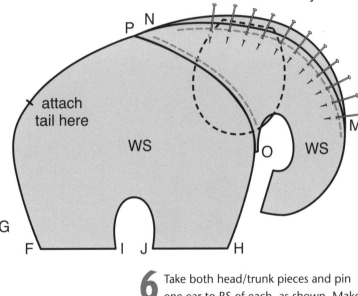

✗ attach tail here

WS

P   N

O   WS

M

F   I   J   H

6 Take both head/trunk pieces and pin one ear to RS of each, as shown. Make sure the contrast lining lies against the RS of the head.

7 Pin the head gusset to the top curve of one side of the head from N to M, including the ear.

8 Repeat, joining the other head/trunk section to the other side of the head gusset.

9 Tack [baste] and then stitch the head to the main body on both sides, from points O to P.

10 Tack [baste] and sew each side of the head gusset from M to N.

11 RS together, sew the body gusset to the body side round the arch from I to J. Clip the curve.

13 Sew down all four legs from points E to F and G to H.

14 Cut three 20 cm [8 in] strands of embroidery thread for the tail. Tie a knot in one end and plait as far as you wish before tying off with a knot and leaving a tassel end.

15 Insert the tail centrally on the back seam, as indicated, with only the base knot sticking out. The rest of the tail should be on the inside for now.

16 Tack [baste] and sew the two body sides together down the spine from P to E. Remove all tacking [basting].

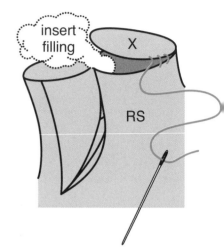

17 Sew the soles of three of the feet into the leg holes, RS facing inwards, matching points H and J, and F and I. With one sole only (see X), sew half the pad to the leg and leave a gap for turning and filling.

18 Turn the whole elephant RS out through the foot hole.

19 Fill firmly, starting with the elephant's trunk. Use a stuffing stick to reach the tip of the trunk and fill it up solidly into the head gusset. The feet and legs should be tightly stuffed too, to avoid sagging where they join the body.

20 Oversew neatly to close the gap in the fourth foot.

21 Attach small black buttons for the eyes.

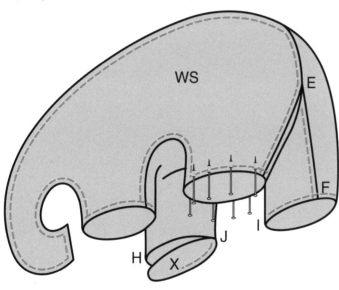

12 Repeat, joining the other body side to the opposite side of the gusset.

ELEPHANT

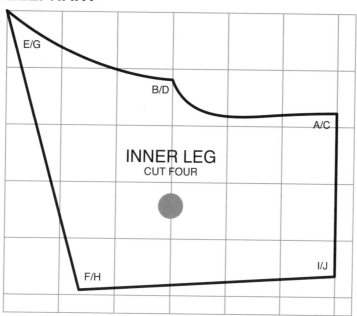

INNER LEG
CUT FOUR

E/G
B/D
A/C
F/H
I/J

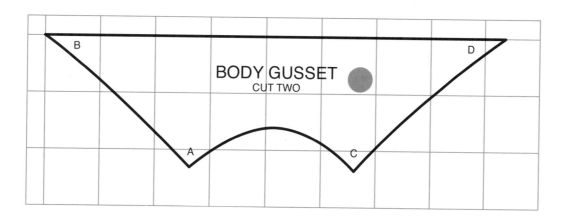

BODY GUSSET
CUT TWO

B
D
A
C

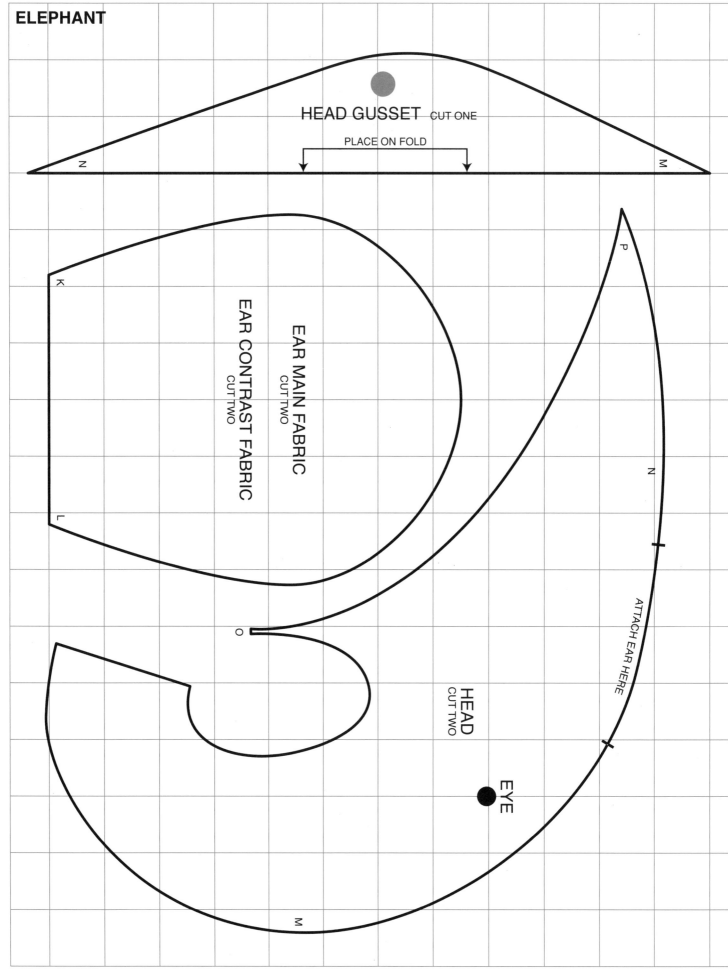

HEAD GUSSET CUT ONE

PLACE ON FOLD

N

M

K

EAR CONTRAST FABRIC CUT TWO

EAR MAIN FABRIC CUT TWO

L

P

N

ATTACH EAR HERE

O

HEAD CUT TWO

EYE

M

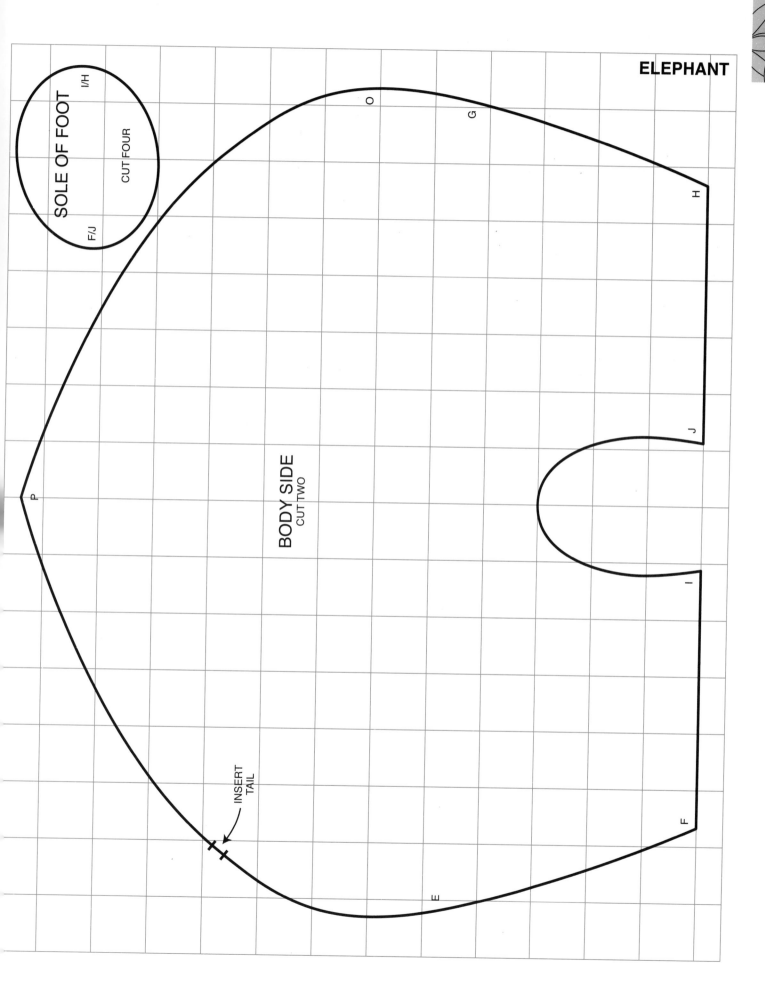

SOLE OF FOOT

I/H

CUT FOUR

F/J

O

G

H

J

I

P

BODY SIDE
CUT TWO

INSERT
TAIL

E

F

PIG

HEIGHT: 14.5 cm [5¾ in] LENGTH: 26 cm [10¼ in]   LEVEL: ADVANCED

Note: This pattern is two-thirds of the original size – for a full-size pig you need to scale up to a 22.5 mm grid (p. 7). Because of the corduroy fabric on the main body, you are advised to use a sewing machine to achieve precise seaming.

YOU WILL NEED

Pink corduroy fabric
60 x 35 cm [24 x 14 in]
for main body

Maroon contrast fabric
50 x 15 cm [19½ x 6 in]
for ears, snout and tail

Two small round black
beads for eyes

Filling

Cut out all the pattern pieces. There is a 5 mm [³⁄₁₆ in] seam allowance.

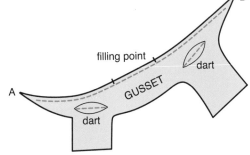

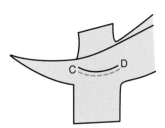

1 Right sides (RS) together, tack [baste] and stitch the leaf-shaped darts closed on both the gusset pieces, C to D and E to F. These curved darts mark the tops of the legs and prevent them from splaying.

2 RS together, join the gusset halves from A to B, leaving a filling gap mid-seam.

3 Sew both ears RS together, leaving the top edge open, and clip the curves. Turn ears RS out.

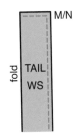

4 Fold the tail in half and sew along the outer edge. Clip the corners and turn RS out.

5 To make sure the ears are level, measure and mark with a line of tacking [basting] before using sharp embroidery scissors to cut slits each side from O to P.

6 Turn cut edges under as you insert the first ear, folded as shown. It's best to hand stitch the ear and slit together neatly, so that no raw edges are left on the RS. Repeat for the other side.

7 Insert tail at B, as shown, and complete the spine seam from B to K.

8 RS together, working from point B to A, tack [baste] and attach the gusset to the two sides of the body, including stitching down all four legs.

9 Insert the four soles of the feet and the snout.

10 Turn the pig RS out through the gap in the gusset.

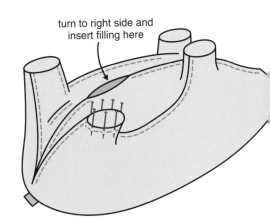

turn to right side and insert filling here

11 Insert the filling very firmly using a stuffing stick, starting with the legs and snout. Slip stitch the filling gap closed.

12 Attach small black beads for the eyes.

13 Tie a knot in the tail.

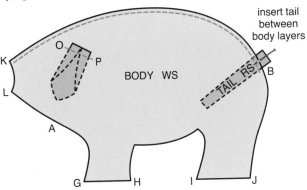

insert tail between body layers

PIG

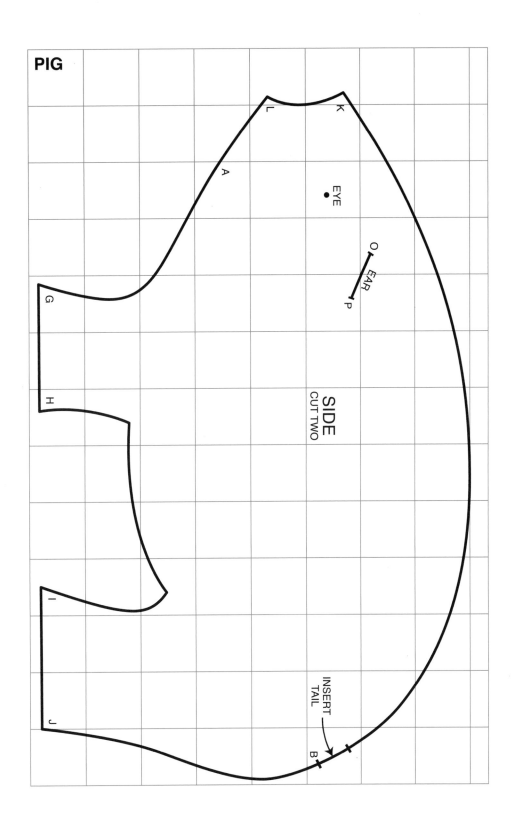

SIDE
CUT TWO

EYE

EAR

O
P

L K

A

G

H

I

J

INSERT
TAIL

B

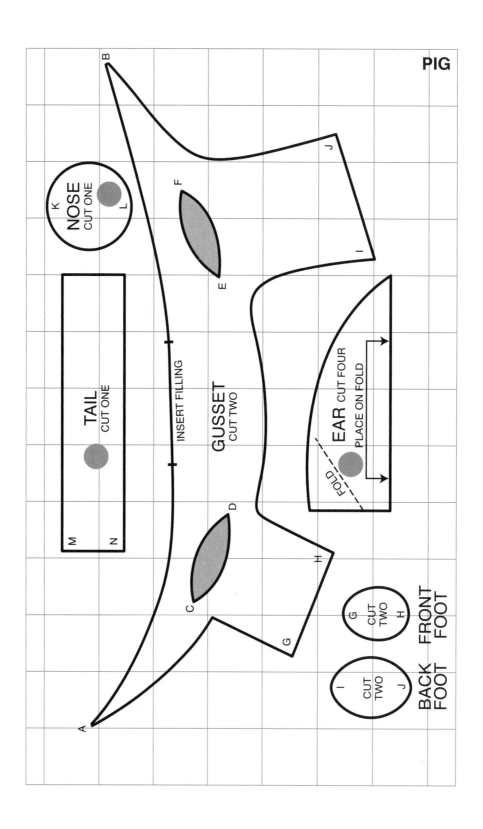

NOSE
CUT ONE
K
L

TAIL
CUT ONE
M
N

INSERT FILLING

GUSSET
CUT TWO

F
E

B

J

I

EAR CUT FOUR
PLACE ON FOLD
FOLD

D
C
H
G

A

G
CUT
TWO
H
FRONT
FOOT

I
CUT
TWO
J
BACK
FOOT

CHINESE BALL

HEIGHT: 9 cm [3½ in]   LEVEL: ADVANCED

Note: You are advised to use a sewing machine. If the ball is made as an ornament rather than a baby's toy, it can be elaborately decorated as in China, where they are made of silk, satin and velvet with embroidery and tassels.

YOU WILL NEED

Close-woven fabric 100 x 20 cm [39 x 8 in] for upper segments (X)

Contrast close-woven fabric 100 x 25 cm [39 x 10 in] for lower segments (Y)

Trimmings such as beads, sequins and tassels, if desired

Filling

Cut out all the pattern pieces. The seam allowance is 3 mm [¹⁄₁₆ in].

1 Right sides (RS) together, stitch two Y pieces to either side of a single X piece.

2 Stitch round each side of Y from A to B, leaving a turning and filling gap of 25 mm [1 in].

insert filling

3 Turn RS out and fill very firmly before slip-stitching the gap closed.

4 Repeat the steps above for the remaining 11 ball segments.

5 Take four segments and sew the tips together, as shown.

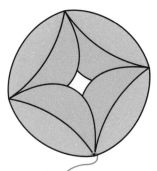

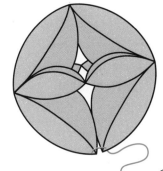

6 Bend all four segments round to form a circle.

7 Link another run of four and create a second circle at a right angle to the first. Join the ends of the second circle together.

8 Linking the last four segments together, create one last chain, which will weave under and over the existing ball, as shown.

9 Make sure the thread loop sits under the other thread loop, so that the next segment sits on top of the next joint.

10 Weave the segments under the next cross section.

11 Leave the last segments to sit above the last cross section.

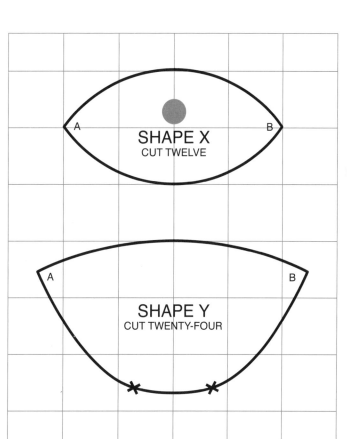

SHAPE X
CUT TWELVE

SHAPE Y
CUT TWENTY-FOUR

12 Secure and complete the entire ball by joining the last two loose segments.

PROJECT: CAT

HEIGHT: 30 cm [12 in]   **LEVEL: ADVANCED**

YOU WILL NEED

Main colour close-woven fabric 60 cm [24 in] square

Contrast close-woven fabric 25 x 20 cm [10 x 8 in] for face, feet and tail

Lightweight scrap fabric (e.g. old T-shirt) 25 x 20 cm [10 x 8 in] for inner bags

Uncooked rice or plastic pellets for inner bags

Black embroidery thread for face, whiskers and paws

Filling

Cut out all the pattern pieces. The seam allowance is 5 mm [³⁄₁₆ in].

1 Take an inner and an outer ear (contrasting colours), put right sides (RS) together and sew from point A through B to C. Turn RS out, using a knitting needle to poke out the points.

2 Sew the contrasting tail tip to the main tail section from D to E. Fold the tail RS together lengthwise, and sew across the top from the fold to point G, then turn and seam the long edge, leaving the tail base open.

3 Turn RS out. Ease closed end over the knob of a knitting needle and work the fabric down until tail tip appears RS out. Grip the tip and pull the rest RS out.

4 Place the face surrounds RS together, pin or tack [baste] and then sew H to I and J to K.

5 Sew darts on the upper and lower face sections, N to O, and P to Q.

6 With RS together, join the upper and lower face from L to M.

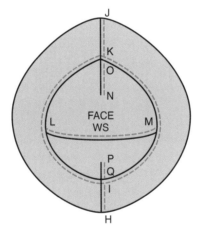

7 Sew the complete face surround to the full face, matching point O to K, and Q to I.

8 RS together, join the two backs of the head from point R to S.

9 Take the face assembly, back of head, and both ears. Position the ears carefully since they define the cat's character. Pin with inner ears facing the face, open ends aligning with the head's outer edge.

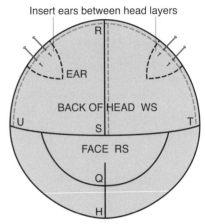

Insert ears between head layers

10 RS together, pin, tack [baste] and sew the back of the head to the front, matching points R and J. Sew from side to side over the top of the head from T to U. Turn head the RS out.

11 RS together, tack [baste] and sew each leg section to the front body from points V to W.

12 Take the two separate back sections of the body and the complete front section. RS together, pin and tack [baste] paws to paws and feet to feet before stitching right down each side from points Y to X.

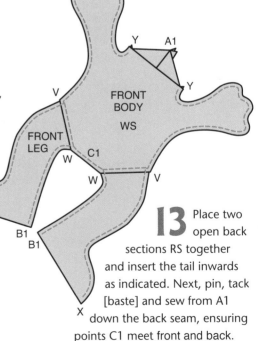

13 Place two open back sections RS together and insert the tail inwards as indicated. Next, pin, tack [baste] and sew from A1 down the back seam, ensuring points C1 meet front and back.

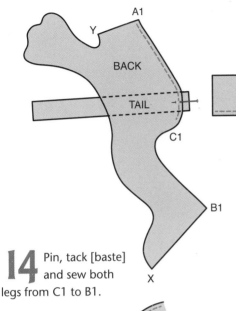

14 Pin, tack [baste] and sew both legs from C1 to B1.

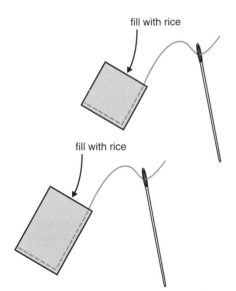

15 Pin, tack [baste] and sew contrasting soles to the open feet so D1 meets X, and D2 meets B1.

16 Turn entire body section RS out.

17 Sew scrap fabric into two small bags, finished size 2.5 cm [1 in] square, for weighting the paws. Do the same, finished size 5 x 2.5 cm [2 x 1 in],

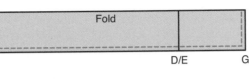

for the feet. Fill with uncooked rice or plastic pellets and stitch each bag closed. Place the two larger bags lengthways inside the feet, and the smaller ones inside the paws.

18 With black embroidery thread, overstitch the paws in the curves between the 'fingers', to a depth of 5 mm [3/16 in]. *Do not stuff either the legs or arms.*

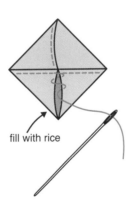

fill with rice

19 Make the pyramid bag from a larger scrap, 10 cm [4 in] square. Fold the points inward to meet in the centre, forming four triangles. Sew the sides together of three triangles, from apex to fold. Fill with rice or pellets through the remaining opening and stitch closed.

20 Placed at the base of the body, the pyramid gives the cat weight and it will sit well. Fill the rest of the body, remembering to leave the limbs empty.

21 Take the cat's head, pin RS together, tack [baste] and stitch to the body around the neckline from T to U. Check the back seam S lines up with A1. Turn the head RS out and stuff firmly.

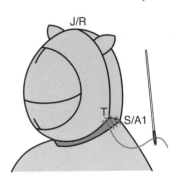

22 With a neat slip stitch and folding in the seam allowance evenly, sew the front of the cat's head to the front of the body.

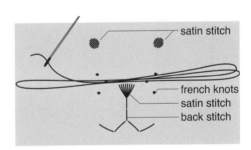

satin stitch

french knots
satin stitch
back stitch

23 Embroider the features using simple embroidery stitches (p. 48) as indicated. Mark them out first with a fabric marker or tacking cotton. If you don't want raised French knots, sew the whisker spots in a tiny star formation. To create the droopy whiskers, double thread your needle and pass through the face from a single whisker dot on one cheek to a matching dot on the other, leaving a long loop each time. Cut the loops then fasten the whiskers with knots close to the dots. Trim if necessary.

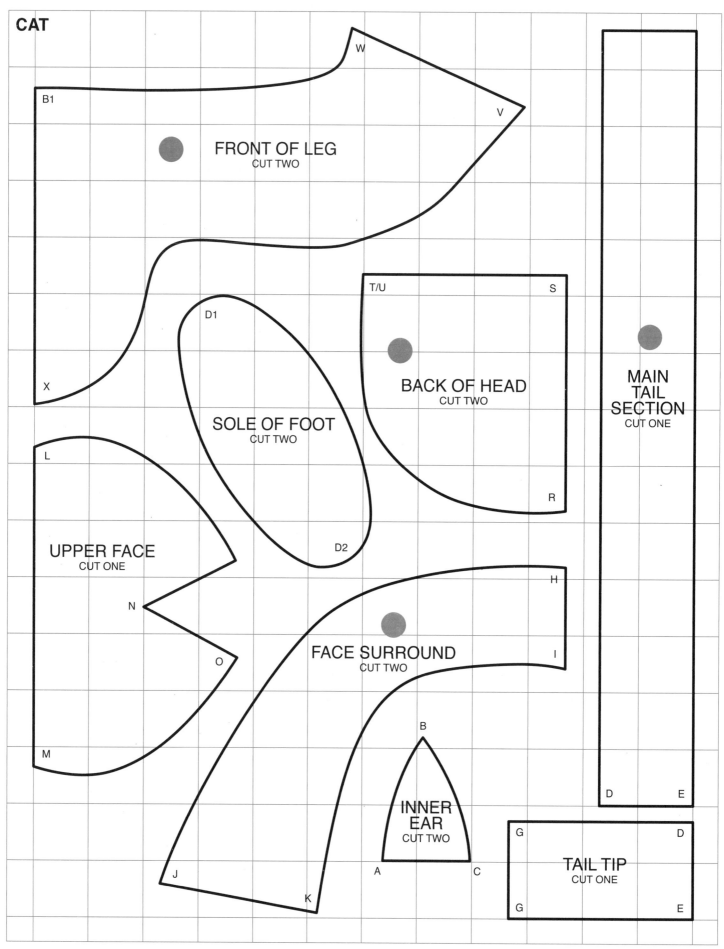

FRONT OF LEG
CUT TWO

B1

W

V

X

D1

SOLE OF FOOT
CUT TWO

D2

T/U

S

BACK OF HEAD
CUT TWO

R

MAIN
TAIL
SECTION
CUT ONE

D

E

L

UPPER FACE
CUT ONE

N

O

M

H

FACE SURROUND
CUT TWO

I

B

INNER
EAR
CUT TWO

A

C

J

K

G

D

TAIL TIP
CUT ONE

G

E

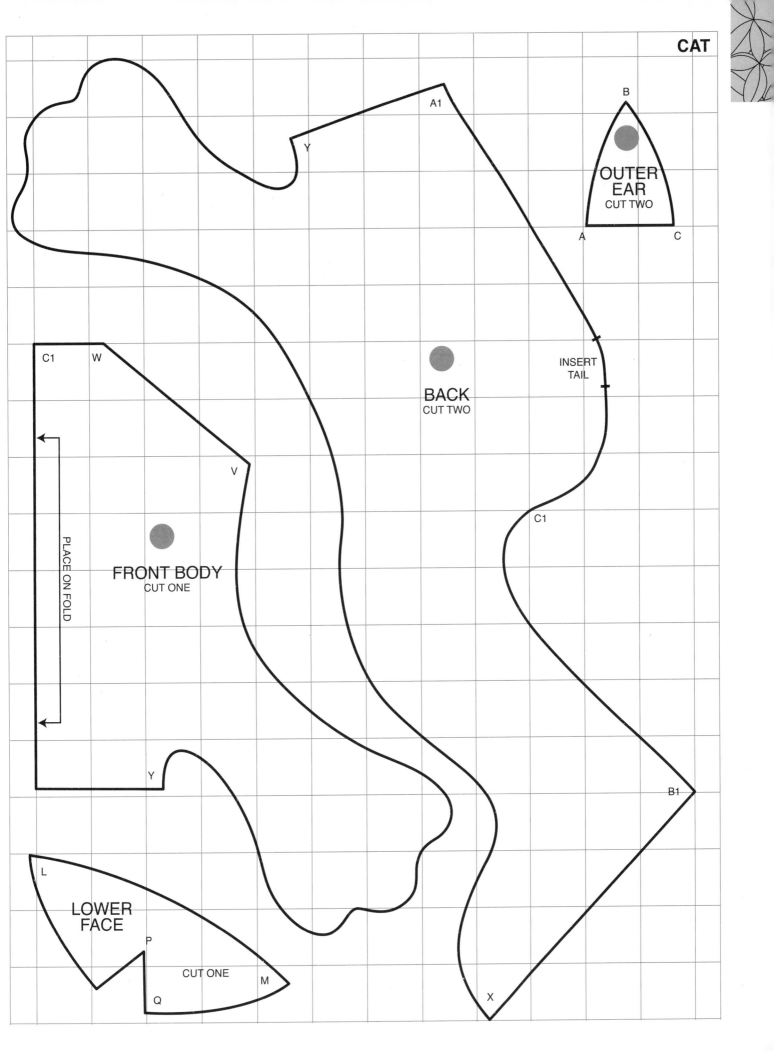

CAT

OUTER
EAR
CUT TWO

B

A   C

BACK
CUT TWO

INSERT
TAIL

C1

A1

Y

C1   W

V

PLACE ON FOLD

FRONT BODY
CUT ONE

Y

B1

LOWER
FACE

L

P

CUT ONE

M

Q

X

RABBIT SNUGGLER

HEIGHT: 32 cm [12½ in]   LEVEL: INTERMEDIATE

YOU WILL NEED

Main colour fleece fabric 100 x 50 cm [39 x 20 in]

Soft satin fabric 60 x 50 cm [24 x 20 in] for lining

Embroidery thread for face, to match lining colour

Filling

Cut out all pattern pieces. The seam allowance is 5 mm [³⁄₁₆ in].

Use the pattern pieces for the cat's head and face (pp. 40–1) in addition to the rabbit's ears and body opposite.

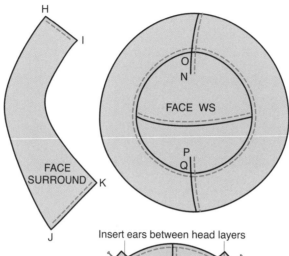

Insert ears between head layers

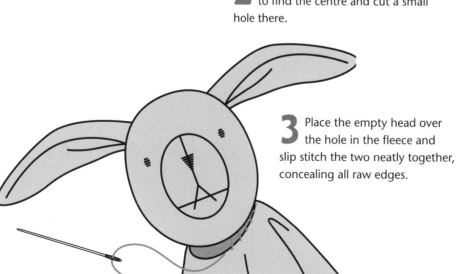

1 Follow the instructions for the cat's head (pp. 42–3) but insert rabbit ears instead of the cat's.

2 Fold the body square into quarters to find the centre and cut a small hole there.

3 Place the empty head over the hole in the fleece and slip stitch the two neatly together, concealing all raw edges.

4 Insert the filling into the head.

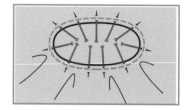

5 Cut a small piece of fleece, about 7 cm [2¾ in] square. Pin over the hole and attach securely over the head/body join to keep the filling in place.

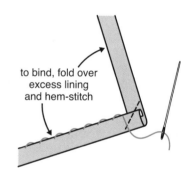

to bind, fold over excess lining and hem-stitch

6 With wrong sides (WS) together, pin and tack [baste] the lining to the fleece square. Fold the lining over to the RS of the fleece square, as shown. Pin, tack [baste] and hem-stitch lining as a decorative bound edge.

7 Embroider the rabbit's face as illustrated. Sleepy eyes with eyelashes are an option.

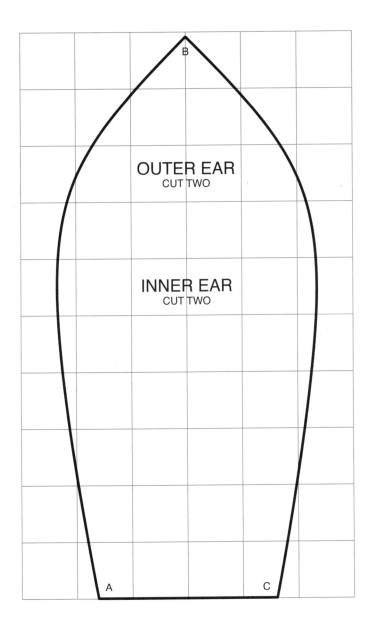

B

OUTER EAR
CUT TWO

INNER EAR
CUT TWO

A   C

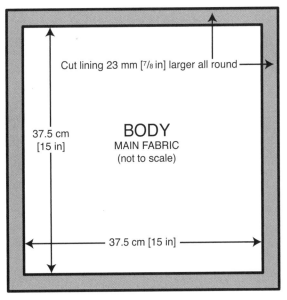

Cut lining 23 mm [7/8 in] larger all round

37.5 cm
[15 in]

BODY
MAIN FABRIC
(not to scale)

37.5 cm [15 in]

TINY TEDDY

HEIGHT: 57 mm [2¼ in] LEVEL: ADVANCED

Note: The tiny teddy is hand-stitched only, using small blanket stitch.

YOU WILL NEED

Very fine flannel fabric (or similar) 20 x 15 cm [8 x 6 in]

Contrast fabric 5 cm [2 in] square for foot pads

Two tiny black beads for eyes

Black or brown stranded embroidery thread for nose and mouth

Filling

Cut out all the pattern pieces. The seam allowance is minimal – it depends solely on the size of your stitching.

ARM

WS

1 Placing right sides (RS) together, stitch the arms, leaving gaps at the top for filling.

2 Turn the arms RS out, and fill firmly before slip stitching closed.

LEG

WS

C   D

3 Placing right sides (RS) together, stitch the legs down each side, leaving gaps at the top for filling.

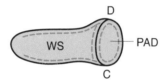

D

WS   PAD

C

4 Insert a foot pad in each leg, matching points C and D.

5 Turn the legs RS out and fill firmly before slip stitching closed.

A

HEAD

B   B

6 RS together, stitch the gusset into the head pieces from A to B on both sides of gusset. Then stitch the head pieces together from point A down to the front neck line.

7 Turn the head RS out and insert filling as firmly as possible but do not close.

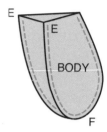

E

E

BODY

F

8 RS together, stitch the body gusset into the body pieces from E to F on both sides of the gusset. Continue to sew the rear body seam from point F up to the back neck line.

9 Turn the body RS out, insert the filling as firmly as possible but do not close.

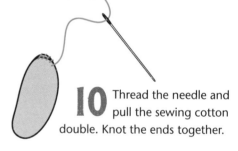

10 Thread the needle and pull the sewing cotton double. Knot the ends together.

11 Attach the arms by stab sewing three times through the body. Bring the needle out between the body and arm and wrap the thread around itself before tying off in a knot.

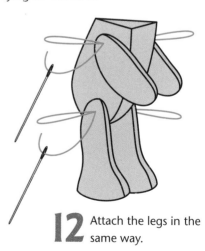

12 Attach the legs in the same way.

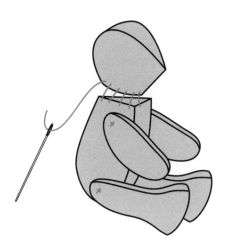

13 Slip stitch the head onto the body. You can add character to your bear by turning the head slightly or inclining it at an angle.

 EAR

14 RS together, sew the ears round from G to H and turn RS out.

15 Attach the ears to the head. Once again, you can add character by setting them at different angles.

16 Sew tiny black beads onto the face for eyes, or embroider with French knots (p. 48).

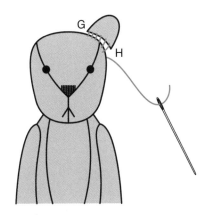

17 Complete the face by embroidering the tiny nose and mouth, as shown.

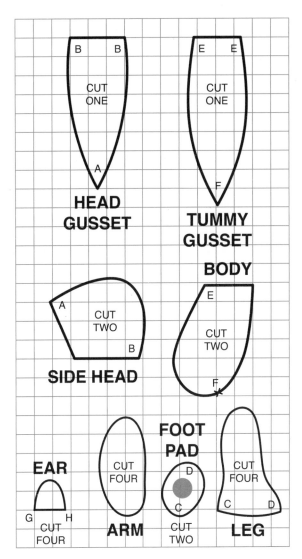

THE GRID ON THIS PATTERN IS ONLY 5 MM [³⁄₁₆ in]

This pattern can be scaled up (p. 7) to produce a traditional teddy of any size. A bigger bear also gives you the chance to work with larger-scale fabrics such as deep pile velvets or fur fabric. (See p. 10 for details of safety eyes.)

For a scaled-up teddy with moveable limbs, you will probably want to use manufactured disc joints. These consist of the main disc and post, a second plain disc, and a washer (p. 10).

Make a small hole with embroidery scissors at the joint position on each pre-filled inner arm or leg, then turn them right sides (RS) out. Push the post section through to the RS of each limb. Insert filling and stitch the limb closed.

Make holes at corresponding joint positions on the pre-filled bear's body, close to the stitching line, then turn the body to RS. Push the post section through each hole from outside to inside the body cavity. Slip the second (plain) disc over each post and fix permanently by pushing a washer down each of the four posts as far as possible. Stuff the bear's body firmly and stitch closed.

USEFUL STITCHES

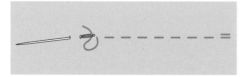

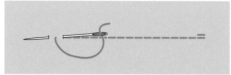

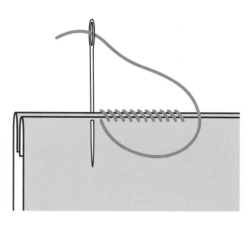

Running stitch Simplest and most basic of stitches, used for seams and gathering. Secure the thread with two small stitches. With the needle at the front, push into the fabric and out again in one move. The stitch and space should be of equal length. Fasten off with a back stitch.

Back stitch Imitates machine stitching. Begin the same as for running stitch then stitch back over the first space. Needle out again at one stitch length ahead of the last stitch made. Repeat with the needle back in again at the point where the previous stitch ended.

Oversewing Used to sew two neatened edges together. Secure the thread with two small stitches and continue with even diagonal stitches, equally spaced.

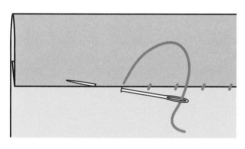

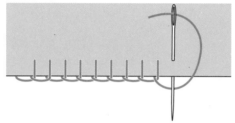

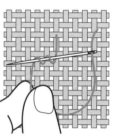

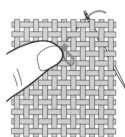

Slip hemming Pick up a few threads of fabric with the needle, enter the fold and slide along inside for up to 1 cm [½ in] before emerging to make the next stitch.

Blanket stitch Secure the thread at the back and bring through at the fabric edge. Needle in from front to back at the desired stitch height and distance to the right. Pass the needle forwards through the loop, forming a half-hitch, and tighten the thread against the fabric edge. Repeat to form a row.

French knot

1 Wrap the thread twice around the needle and pull gently to tighten the coils towards the tip.

2 Insert the needle near the exit point and with your thumb on coils, pull the thread gently but firmly through the fabric, leaving a knot upon the surface.

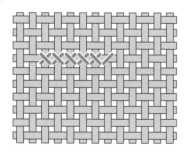

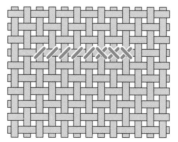

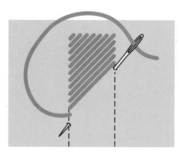

Cross stitch The traditional English method (left) completes each X before moving on to the next. The Danish method (right) stitches one leg of the Xs first, and completes them on a return pass.

Satin stitch Work satin stitches very closely together to cover the base fabric completely. Needle in and out at the same angle within a defined outline.